W9-CPF-637

Frightfully Fun
HALLOWEEN
Recipes

Happy Halloween!

Critter Cubes

Keep drinks cold with ice cubes that show Halloween spirit! Fill an ice cube tray half full of water; freeze. Place a small gummy creature or piece of candy corn on each ice cube. Cover with water and freeze until completely frozen.

Monster Masks

For any Halloween party, costumes are required but you may want to make festive masks as one of the party activities. Provide a plain mask (either purchased or cut out from poster board or paper plates) for each child and supply paints, markers, colored papers, fabric, yarn and glitter. Stickers are also an easy way to decorate. Give prizes for the scariest, prettiest or most creative—just be sure every child wins something.

Make Halloween A Scream!

◆ Create scary decorations like cobwebs and bats and hang them from the ceiling.

◆ Turn down the lights and play a recording of scary sounds to add to the spooky atmosphere.

◆ Place a life-sized skeleton inside a closet and decorate with cobwebs. Entice guests into opening the door by hanging a "Do Not Enter" sign on the doorknob.

Spooky Spiderwebs Game

For this game, you'll need a different colored ball of yarn for each team. Before the party begins, tie prizes for each team at the end of each ball of yarn and hide the prize. Then unwind the yarn around a room—around the furniture, under tables, behind the sofa—creating a spiderweb of yarn. When the party starts, pass out the loose ends of yarn to the teams. Have them wind the yarn back up into a ball, following it around the room until they find their prizes.

Ghostly Favors

Little monsters will adore these party favors!

◆ Place some small candies in a sandwich bag for the head. Secure the ball tightly with tape.

◆ Drape a napkin over the head and tie a ribbon tightly around the neck.

◆ Draw a face on the ghost.

Haunted Mobile

Cut out Halloween shapes from colored foam or poster board and decorate with wiggle eyes and markers. Along the bottom of the main center piece, punch one hole for each dangling piece. Punch one hole in the tops of the dangling pieces and in the top of the main piece. Attach the dangling pieces to the main piece with different lengths of ribbon.

No Tricks — Just Treats!

Make an extra-sturdy trick or treat bag from a canvas tote bag. For a spirited jack-o'-lantern, cut out a pumpkin shape from orange felt, a nose and mouth from yellow or black felt, and a stem and a few leaves from green felt. Using fabric glue, attach wiggle eyes and the nose and mouth to the pumpkin shape. Glue the jack-o'-lantern to the tote bag and then glue on the leaves.

Graveyard Grub

Mummy Dogs

1 package (8 breadsticks or 11 ounces) breadstick dough
1 package (16 ounces) hot dogs
  Mustard and poppy seeds

◆ Preheat oven to 375°F. Using 1 dough strip for each, wrap hot dogs to look like mummies, leaving opening for eyes. Place on ungreased baking sheet.

◆ Bake 12 to 15 minutes or until light golden brown. Place dots of mustard and poppy seeds for eyes.

Makes 8 servings

Mini Mummy Dogs: Use 1 package (16 ounces) mini hot dogs instead of regular hot dogs. Cut each breadstick strip into 3 pieces. Cut each piece in half lengthwise. Using 1 strip of dough for each, wrap and bake mini hot dogs as directed above.

Mummy Dogs

Grilled Cheese Jack-O'-Lanterns

3 tablespoons butter or margarine, softened
8 slices bread
4 slices Monterey Jack cheese
4 slices sharp Cheddar cheese

◆ Preheat oven to 350°F. Spread butter on one side of each bread slice. Place bread buttered-side-down on ungreased cookie sheet.

◆ Using small sharp hors d'oeuvre cutter or knife, cut out shapes from 4 bread slices to make jack-o'-lantern faces. On remaining bread slices layer 1 slice Monterey Jack and 1 slice Cheddar.

◆ Bake 10 to 12 minutes or until cheese is melted. Remove from oven; place jack-o'-lantern bread slice on sandwiches and serve.
Makes 4 servings

Bat & Spook Pizzas

4 (6-inch) Italian bread shells
⅔ cup pizza or spaghetti sauce
1 package (3½ ounces) pepperoni slices
4 slices (1 ounce each) mozzarella cheese

◆ Preheat oven to 375°F. Place bread shells on ungreased baking sheet.

◆ Spread pizza sauce evenly on bread shells; top evenly with pepperoni slices.

◆ Cut out ghost and bat shapes from cheese slices with cookie cutters; place on pizza sauce.

◆ Bake 10 to 12 minutes or until cheese is melted.
Makes 4 servings

Top to bottom: Grilled Cheese Jack-O'-Lanterns and Potato Bugs (page 34)

Eyes of Newt

2 cans (2¼ ounces
    each) sliced ripe
    olives, divided
¼ cup chopped roasted
    red pepper, divided
1 package (8 ounces)
    cream cheese,
    softened
1 clove garlic, minced
8 (6- to 7-inch) flour
    tortillas
16 slices deli roast beef

◆ Reserve 48 olive slices,
48 pieces red pepper and 1
tablespoon cream cheese.

◆ Chop remaining olives.
Combine remaining cream
cheese, olives, red pepper
and garlic in small bowl; mix
well.

◆ Spread about 2
tablespoons cream cheese
mixture on each tortilla. Top
each tortilla with 2 beef
slices, overlapping slightly.
Roll up tortillas, jelly-roll
fashion. Trim off uneven
ends of each tortilla; discard.
Slice each tortilla roll into 6
(¾-inch) pieces.

◆ Using reserved cream
cheese, attach reserved
olives and red pepper to
make roll-ups look like eyes.
Makes 4 dozen pieces

Give your guests goosebumps
when you present "A Ghost's
Tale." Turn off all the lights
and then read a spine-tingling
story by candlelight or
flashlight. Have another adult
or older child behind the party
guests, making eerie sound
effects to go with the story.

*Top to bottom: Cheesy Bat
Biscuits (page 27) and
Eyes of Newt*

Halloween Chicken Pizza Masks

1 pound ground chicken
½ cup chopped onion
1 teaspoon salt
1 teaspoon dried oregano leaves
½ teaspoon ground black pepper
6 English muffins, split
1½ cups prepared pizza sauce
1 large green or red bell pepper
1 cup (4 ounces) shredded Cheddar cheese
1 cup (4 ounces) shredded mozzarella cheese
1 can (2¼ ounces) sliced black olives, drained

Heat large skillet over medium-high heat until hot. Add chicken, onion, salt, oregano and black pepper. Cook and stir about 6 minutes or until chicken is no longer pink; set aside. Cover 15½×10½-inch baking pan with foil. Arrange muffins in single layer on prepared pan. Spread 2 tablespoons pizza sauce on each muffin half. Cover generously with chicken mixture, dividing evenly. Cut 12 slivers bell pepper into "smiling" mouth shapes; set aside. Chop remaining bell pepper; sprinkle over mini-pizzas. Combine Cheddar and mozzarella cheeses in small bowl; sprinkle generously over mini-pizzas. Bake at 450°F 12 minutes or until cheese is light brown. Make face on each pizza by using 2 olive slices for "eyes" and 1 pepper shape for "mouth."

Makes 12 mini-pizzas

*Favorite recipe from **National Chicken Council***

Halloween Chicken Pizza Masks

Salsa Macaroni & Cheese

1 jar (16 ounces) RAGÚ® Cheese Creations!® Double Cheddar Sauce
1 cup prepared mild salsa
8 ounces elbow macaroni, cooked and drained

1. In 2-quart saucepan, heat Ragú Cheese Creations! Sauce over medium heat. Stir in salsa; heat through.

2. Toss with hot macaroni. Serve immediately.
Makes 4 servings

Prep Time: 5 minutes
Cook Time: 15 minutes

Peanut Pitas

1 package (8 ounces) small pita breads, cut crosswise in half
16 teaspoons reduced-fat peanut butter
16 teaspoons strawberry spreadable fruit
1 large banana, peeled and thinly sliced (about 48 slices)

◆ Spread inside of each pita half with 1 teaspoon each peanut butter and spreadable fruit.

◆ Fill pita halves evenly with banana slices. Serve immediately.
Makes 8 servings

Honey Bees: Substitute honey for spreadable fruit.

Jolly Jellies: Substitute any flavor jelly for spreadable fruit and thin apple slices for banana slices.

Salsa Macaroni & Cheese

Monster Claws

2 tablespoons flour
1 tablespoon plus
    2 teaspoons cajun
    seasoning, divided
1 pound boneless
    skinless chicken
    breasts, cut
    lengthwise into
    ¾-inch strips
1½ cups cornflake
    crumbs
2 tablespoons chopped
    green onion
3 eggs, lightly beaten
1 red, yellow or orange
    bell pepper, cut
    into triangles
Barbecue sauce

◆ Preheat oven to 350°F. Lightly grease baking sheets. Place flour and 2 teaspoons cajun seasoning in large resealable plastic food storage bag. Add chicken and seal. Shake bag to coat.

◆ Combine cornflake crumbs, green onion and remaining 1 tablespoon cajun seasoning in large shallow bowl; mix well. Place eggs in shallow bowl.

◆ Dip each chicken strip into eggs and then into crumb mixture. Place coated chicken strips on prepared baking sheet.

◆ Bake chicken strips 8 to 10 minutes or until chicken is no longer pink in center.

◆ When chicken is cool enough to handle, make ½-inch slit in thinner end. Place bell pepper triangle into slit to form claw nail. Serve claws with barbecue sauce for dipping.
Makes about 30 strips

A bewitching way to garnish a Halloween dish is with vegetable cutouts! Use a small metal cookie cutter or sharp knife to cut Halloween shapes from bell peppers, carrots, parsnips, squash, eggplant or tomatoes.

Monster Claws

Harvest Sticks with Vegetable Dip

2 packages (3 ounces each) cream cheese with chives, softened
1 cup sour cream
⅓ cup finely chopped cucumber
2 tablespoons chopped fresh parsley
2 tablespoons dry minced onion
1 clove garlic, minced
¼ teaspoon salt
½ teaspoon curry powder (optional)
6 large carrots, peeled
3 medium zucchini

SUPPLIES
Tan raffia

◆ Beat cream cheese in small bowl until fluffy; blend in sour cream. Stir in cucumber, parsley, onion, garlic and salt. Add curry powder, if desired. Spoon into small serving bowl; cover. Refrigerate 1 hour or until serving time.

◆ Just before serving, cut carrots lengthwise into thin strips; gather into bundles. Tie raffia around bundles to hold in place. Repeat with zucchini.

◆ Place bowl of dip on serving tray; garnish, if desired. Surround with vegetable bundles.
Makes 2 cups dip

These vegetable bundles can be made ahead of time. Cut up the vegetables as directed. Place the carrots in a medium bowl; cover with cold water. Place the zucchini sticks in a small resealable plastic food storage bag. Refrigerate the vegetables until ready to use. Just before serving, tie them into bundles as directed.

Left to right: Pumpkin Yeast Rolls (page 22) and Harvest Sticks with Vegetable Dip

Pumpkin Yeast Rolls

- 16 slivered almonds
- 1/4 teaspoon green food color
- 1 package (16 ounces) hot roll mix
- 1 to 1 1/4 teaspoons pumpkin pie spice
- 2/3 cup apple cider
- 1/3 cup warm water
- 2 tablespoons butter, softened
- 1 whole egg, slightly beaten
- 1 egg white
- 2 tablespoons cold water

1. Place almonds in small resealable plastic food storage bag. Add food color; seal bag. Shake bag until almonds are evenly colored. Place almonds on paper-towel-lined plate; let dry.

2. Combine hot roll mix, yeast package from mix and pumpkin pie spice in large bowl; stir to mix well.

3. Combine cider and warm water in small saucepan. Heat over medium heat until cider mixture is hot (120° to 130°F); pour over dry ingredients. Add butter and whole egg; stir until dough pulls away from side of bowl.

4. Place dough on lightly floured surface; knead until smooth and elastic, about 5 minutes. Let rest 5 minutes. Cut dough into 16 equal pieces; roll each piece into ball. Combine egg white and cold water in small bowl; beat lightly with fork until well blended.

5. Brush egg white mixture evenly onto rolls, covering completely.

6. With sharp knife, lightly score surface of each roll, beginning at top center and coming down around sides of roll, to resemble pumpkin. Insert 1 almond sliver into top of each roll for stem.

7. Lightly grease baking sheet. Place rolls 2 inches apart on prepared baking sheet. Cover loosely with towel; let rise in warm place 20 to 30 minutes or until doubled in size. Remove towel.

8. Preheat oven to 375°F. Bake 15 to 20 minutes or until golden brown.

Makes 16 rolls

Individual Mashed Potato Ghosts

5 cups mashed Idaho Potatoes
Waxed paper
½ cup small black olives

1. Cut ghost shapes out of waxed paper to use as templates.

2. Place templates on serving dish or cookie sheet. Use rubber spatula to mold ½ to 1 cup potatoes into each ghost shape.

3. Slice olives to create circular shapes to be used for eyes and mouth.
Makes 4 to 6 servings

Note: To warm Individual Mashed Potato Ghosts, microwave on HIGH 2 to 4 minutes on microwavable plate. If using oven, place potatoes on cookie sheet and re-heat at 350°F, loosely covered with foil, 7 to 8 minutes or until heated through.

*Favorite recipe from **Idaho Potato Commission***

Western Wagon Wheels

1 pound lean ground beef or ground turkey
2 cups wagon wheel pasta, uncooked
1 can (14½ ounces) stewed tomatoes
1½ cups water
1 box (10 ounces) BIRDS EYE® frozen Sweet Corn
½ cup barbecue sauce
Salt and pepper to taste

◆ In large skillet, cook beef over medium heat 5 minutes or until well browned.

◆ Stir in pasta, tomatoes, water, corn and barbecue sauce; bring to a boil.

◆ Reduce heat to low; cover and simmer 15 to 20 minutes or until pasta is tender, stirring occasionally. Season with salt and pepper.
Makes 4 servings

Serving Suggestion: Serve with corn bread or corn muffins.

Bewitching Bites

Spider Web Dip

Spooky Tortilla Chips (page 26)
1 package (8 ounces) cream cheese, softened
1 jar (8 ounces) prepared salsa
½ cup prepared guacamole
2 tablespoons sour cream

◆ Prepare Spooky Tortilla Chips; set aside.

◆ Place cream cheese and salsa in blender or food processor container; blend until almost smooth.

◆ Spread cream cheese mixture on round serving dish or pie plate; smooth guacamole over top, leaving ½-inch border.

continued on page 26

Spider Web Dip

Spider Web Dip, continued

◆ Place sour cream in small resealable plastic food storage bag; seal bag. Cut off tiny corner of bag; pipe sour cream in several circles over guacamole. Run tip of knife through sour cream to make "spider web." Serve with Spooky Tortilla Chips.

Makes 10 servings

Spooky Tortilla Chips

3 packages (12 ounces each) 8-inch plain or flavored flour tortillas
Salt to taste

◆ Preheat oven to 350°F. Spray baking sheet with olive oil nonstick cooking spray.

◆ Using 3-inch Halloween cookie cutters, cut tortillas, one at a time, into shapes. Discard scraps.

◆ Lightly spray tortilla shapes with cooking spray. Place on prepared baking sheet and sprinkle with salt.

◆ Bake 5 to 7 minutes or until edges begin to brown. Remove to wire rack to cool completely.

Makes about 90 chips

Magic Dip

1 package (8 ounces) PHILADELPHIA® Cream Cheese, softened
1 cup BAKER'S® Semi-Sweet Real Chocolate Chips
½ cup BAKER'S® ANGEL FLAKE® Coconut, toasted
½ cup chopped peanuts
Graham crackers

SPREAD cream cheese on bottom of 9-inch microwavable pie plate or quiche dish.

TOP with remaining ingredients except graham crackers.

MICROWAVE on MEDIUM (50% power) 3 to 4 minutes or until warm. Serve with graham crackers. Garnish, if desired.

Makes 6 to 8 servings

Prep Time: 5 minutes
Microwave Time: 4 minutes

Cheesy Bat Biscuits

1 can (16 ounces)
    jumbo refrigerated
    buttermilk biscuits
3 tablespoons butter,
    melted and divided
¼ cup grated Parmesan
    cheese
1 teaspoon dried
    parsley flakes
1 teaspoon dried basil
    leaves

◆ Preheat oven to 350°F.

◆ Flatten each biscuit into shape just large enough to fit 3-inch bat cookie cutter. Cut out bat shape; discard scraps. Place biscuits on baking sheet. Lightly score biscuits to outline bat wings; poke holes with toothpick for eyes. Brush biscuits with 1 tablespoon butter. Bake 7 minutes.

◆ Meanwhile, combine cheese, remaining 2 tablespoons butter, parsley and basil in small bowl.

◆ Turn biscuits on end and split into halves with forks. Spread 1 teaspoon cheese mixture on bottom half of each biscuit; replace biscuit top. Bake 3 minutes or until biscuits are golden brown.

Makes 8 servings

Haunted Hint

Halloween is the perfect time to have a theme party! Choose a theme that has a wide variety of costume options, such as "A Trip to the Zoo," "Under the Sea" or "The Insect World." Make the invitations, food, decorations, and even the games reflect the theme.

Creepy Hands

8 cups popped popcorn
1 cup pumpkin seeds, cleaned and patted dry
⅓ cup butter or margarine, melted
1 tablespoon Worcestershire sauce
½ teaspoon garlic salt
½ teaspoon seasoned salt
Candy corn

SUPPLIES
6 clear industrial food handler's gloves
Orange and/or black ribbon
6 plastic spider rings

◆ Preheat oven to 300°F. Place popcorn in single layer in 15×10×1-inch jelly-roll pan; sprinkle pumpkin seeds evenly over top.

◆ Combine butter, Worcestershire sauce, garlic salt and seasoned salt in small bowl; mix well. Pour over popcorn; toss lightly to evenly coat.

◆ Bake 30 minutes, stirring after 15 minutes. Cool completely in pan on wire rack.

◆ Place candy corn in end of each glove finger for fingernail; pack glove tightly with popcorn mixture. Close bag tightly at wrist; tie with ribbon. Place ring on 1 finger of each hand.

Makes 6 servings

Set a creepy table for your party! For each guest, roll up a paper napkin and use a plastic spider ring as a napkin ring.

Clockwise from top left: Chocolate Spiders (page 87), Monster Eyes (page 30), Doughnut Hole Spider (page 87) and Creepy Hand

Witches' Brew

2 cups apple cider
1½ to 2 cups vanilla ice
   cream
2 tablespoons honey
½ teaspoon ground
   cinnamon
¼ teaspoon ground
   nutmeg

Process cider, ice cream,
honey, cinnamon and
nutmeg in food processor or
blender until smooth. Pour
into glasses and sprinkle
with additional nutmeg.
Serve immediately.
Makes 4 servings

Serving Suggestion: Add a
few drops of desired food
coloring to ingredients in
food processor to make a
scary brew.

Lighten Up: To reduce fat,
replace vanilla ice cream
with reduced-fat or fat-free
ice cream or frozen yogurt.

Monster Eyes

1 container (8 ounces)
   plain soft cream
   cheese
6 miniature bagels,
   split and toasted
6 midget sweet pickles
   Red decorating icing

◆ Spread cream cheese
evenly onto toasted bagels,
leaving center holes in
bagels unfrosted.

◆ Cut pickles crosswise in
half; insert, cut sides up, into
bagel holes. Use icing to add
"veins" and "pupils" to eyes.
*Makes 12 appetizer
servings*

Witches' Brew

Jack-O'-Lantern Cheese Ball

2 cups (8 ounces) shredded Cheddar cheese
½ (8-ounce) package cream cheese, softened
¼ cup solid pack pumpkin
¼ cup pineapple preserves
¼ teaspoon ground allspice
¼ teaspoon ground nutmeg
1 pretzel rod, broken in half
Dark rye bread, red bell pepper and black olive slices
Assorted crackers

◆ Beat cheeses, pumpkin, preserves and spices in medium bowl until smooth. Cover; refrigerate 2 to 3 hours or until cheese is firm enough to shape.

◆ Shape mixture into round pumpkin; place on serving plate. Using knife, score vertical lines down pumpkin.

◆ Place pretzel rod in top for stem. Cut bread into triangles for eyes. Decorate as shown.

◆ Cover loosely; refrigerate until serving time. Serve with crackers.
Makes 18 servings

For a traditional costume party, complete with vampires, ghosts and goblins, make a haunted house or coffin invitation. First fold a piece of black paper in half. Cut out a house or coffin shape without cutting the fold on the left side. Next cut out a ghost or mummy shape from white paper to fit inside the house or coffin. Write the party information on the ghost or mummy.

Jack-O'-Lantern Cheese Ball

Hot Cocoa with Floating Eyeballs

16 large marshmallows
16 black licorice candies
2 quarts milk
1 cup chocolate-flavored drink mix
1 cup mint-flavored semisweet chocolate chips

SUPPLIES
16 lollipop sticks

◆ Make slit in center of each marshmallow; insert candy into slit. Insert lollipop stick into center of bottom of each eyeball; set aside.

◆ Combine milk and drink mix in medium saucepan. Stir in chocolate chips. Cook over medium heat, stirring occasionally, until chips are melted and milk is hot.

◆ Place 2 eyeballs in each mug; fill mug with hot cocoa. Serve immediately.
Makes 8 servings

Potato Bugs

1 package (16 ounces) shredded potato nuggets
6 pieces uncooked spaghetti, broken into thirds
1 carrot, cut into 1½-inch strips
Sour cream, black olive slices, ketchup and broccoli pieces

◆ Preheat oven to 450°F. Lightly grease baking sheets. Spread potato nuggets on baking sheets. Bake 7 minutes. Loosen nuggets from baking sheets.

◆ Thread 3 potato nuggets onto 1 spaghetti piece. Bake 5 minutes. Carefully push carrot strips into sides of each nugget for legs. Using sour cream to attach vegetables, decorate faces.
Makes 15 servings

Clockwise from top left:
Chocolate-Dipped Caramel
Apples (page 61), Hot Cocoa
with Floating Eyeballs and
Tombstone Place Cards
(page 69)

Magic Potion

Creepy Crawler Ice
Ring (recipe
follows)
1 cup boiling water
2 packages (4-serving
size each) lime-
flavored gelatin
3 cups cold water
1½ quarts carbonated
lemon-lime
beverage, chilled
½ cup superfine sugar
Gummy worms
(optional)

◆ One day ahead, prepare
Creepy Crawler Ice Ring.

◆ Pour boiling water over
gelatin in heatproof punch
bowl; stir until gelatin
dissolves. Stir in cold water.
Add lemon-lime beverage
and sugar; stir well (mixture
will foam for a few minutes).

◆ Unmold ice ring by
dipping bottom of mold
briefly into hot water. Float
ice ring in punch. Serve
cups of punch garnished
with gummy worms, if
desired.

Makes 10 servings

Creepy Crawler Ice Ring

1 cup gummy worms
or other creepy
crawler candy
1 quart lemon-lime
thirst quencher
beverage

◆ Arrange gummy worms in
bottom of 5-cup ring mold;
fill mold with thirst
quencher beverage. Freeze
until solid, 8 hours or
overnight.

Change this Magic Potion from
creepy to cute with just a few
simple substitutions. For the
punch, use orange-flavored
gelatin instead of lime. For the
ice ring, use candy corn and
candy pumpkins instead of
gummy worms.

Magic Potion

Eyeballs

12 hard-cooked eggs
1 can (4½ ounces)
    deviled ham
⅓ cup mayonnaise
4 teaspoons prepared
    mustard
¼ cup drained sweet
    pickle relish
12 pimiento-stuffed
    olives, halved
    Ketchup

◆ Cut eggs lengthwise into halves. Remove yolks; place in small bowl. Mash egg yolks with fork; mix in deviled ham, mayonnaise, mustard and pickle relish. Season to taste with salt and pepper.

◆ Spoon filling into egg halves. Garnish with olive halves to make "eyeballs."

◆ To make bloodshot "eyeballs," spoon ketchup into small resealable plastic food storage bag. Cut off tiny corner of bag; drizzle over eggs.

Makes 12 servings

Cutting Corners: To save time, use leftover ketchup packets to drizzle over eggs to make bloodshot "eyeballs."

Cinnamon Apple Chips

2 cups unsweetened
    apple juice
1 cinnamon stick
2 Washington Red
    Delicious apples

1. In large skillet, mix juice and cinnamon stick; bring to a low boil. Slice off ½ inch from tops and bottoms of apples; discard. Stand apples on one cut end; slice crosswise ⅛ inch thick.

2. Drop slices into boiling juice; cook 4 to 5 minutes or until slices are translucent and lightly golden. Preheat oven to 250°F.

3. Remove apple slices from juice; pat dry. Arrange slices on wire racks, being sure none overlap. Place racks on middle shelf in oven. Bake slices 30 to 40 minutes until lightly browned and almost dry to touch. Cool on racks. Store in airtight container.
    Makes about 40 chips

Favorite recipe from
Washington Apple Commission

Eyeballs

Trick-or-Treat Punch

Green food color
1 envelope (4 ounces) orange-flavored presweetened drink mix
1 can (12 ounces) frozen lemonade concentrate, thawed
1 bottle (2 liters) ginger ale*

SUPPLIES
1 new plastic household glove

*For an adult party, substitute 2 bottles (750 ml each) champagne for ginger ale, if desired.

◆ One day ahead, fill pitcher with 3 cups water; color with green food color. Pour into glove; tightly secure top of glove with twist tie. Line baking sheet with paper towels; place glove on prepared baking sheet. Use inverted custard cup to elevate tied end of glove to prevent leaking. Freeze overnight.

◆ When ready to serve, combine drink mix, lemonade concentrate and 4 cups water in large bowl; stir until drink mix is dissolved and mixture is well blended. Pour into punch bowl; add ginger ale.

◆ Cut glove away from ice; float frozen hand in punch.
Makes 16 (6-ounce) servings and 1 ice hand

Make this punch a ghoulish centerpiece. Serve the punch, with the ice hand, in a large plastic black cauldron. Then surround it with an array of spooky treats.

Top to bottom: Trick-or-Treat Punch and Orange Jack-O'-Lanterns (page 80)

Ghost on a Stick

4 wooden craft sticks
4 medium pears, stems removed
9 squares (2 ounces each) almond bark
Mini chocolate chips

◆ Line baking sheet with waxed paper and 4 paper baking cups. Insert wooden sticks into stem ends of pears. Melt bark according to package directions. Dip pear into bark, spooning over top to coat. Remove excess by scraping pear bottom across rim of measuring cup. Place on baking cup; let set 1 minute. Decorate with chocolate chips. Repeat with remaining pears. Place spoonful of extra bark at bottom of pears for ghost tails. Chill until firm. *Makes 4 servings*

Left to right: Monster Munch (page 68) and Ghost on a Stick

Tricky Treats 44 Tricky Treats

Little Devils

1 package (18 ounces)
   carrot cake mix
½ cup solid pack
   pumpkin
⅓ cup vegetable oil
3 eggs
1 tub (16 ounces)
   cream cheese
   frosting
   Assorted Halloween
   candies, jelly
   beans, chocolate
   candies and nuts

◆ Preheat oven to 350°F.
Prepare cake mix according
to package directions, using
water as directed on
package, pumpkin, oil and
eggs. Spoon batter into 18
paper-lined muffin cups.
Bake 20 minutes or until
toothpick inserted in
centers of cupcakes comes
out clean. Cool in pans on
wire rack 5 minutes; remove
and cool completely.

◆ Frost cupcakes with
frosting. Let each goblin
guest decorate his own
cupcake with assorted
candies.

Makes 18 cupcakes

Spiders

1 (3-inch) oatmeal
   cookie
1 tablespoon Fluffy
   White Frosting
   (recipe follows)
1 small black jelly bean
1 large black jelly bean
1 black licorice whip
2 red candy-coated
   licorice pieces

Frost oatmeal cookie with
Fluffy White Frosting.
Arrange jelly beans on
cookies to make spider head
and body. Cut 6 to 8 licorice
whip pieces (about 1½
inches long); curve and
position for legs. Add red
candy antennae to head.
Makes 1 cookie

Fluffy White Frosting:
Combine 1 (16-ounce) tub
vanilla frosting and ¾ cup
marshmallow creme in
medium bowl; mix well.
Makes about 2 cups.

Full-Moon Pumpkin Cheesecake

Gingersnap Cookie
Crust (page 50)
4 packages (8 ounces
  each) cream
  cheese, softened
½ cup sugar
6 eggs
1 cup sour cream
1 cup solid pack
  pumpkin
2 tablespoons all-
  purpose flour
2 teaspoons ground
  cinnamon
½ teaspoon ground
  ginger
½ teaspoon ground
  allspice
3 ounces semisweet
  chocolate, melted
1 recipe Black Cat
  Fudge (page 51)

◆ Prepare Gingersnap Cookie Crust; set aside.

◆ *Increase oven temperature to 425°F.* Beat cream cheese in large bowl until fluffy; beat in sugar and eggs, one at a time. Add sour cream, pumpkin, flour and spices; beat well. Pour 2 cups batter into small bowl; stir in chocolate.

◆ Pour remaining batter into prepared crust. Spoon chocolate batter in large swirls over batter in pan; draw knife through mixture to marbleize.

◆ Bake 15 minutes. *Reduce oven temperature to 300°F.* Bake 45 minutes (center of cheesecake will not be set). Turn oven off; let cheesecake stand in oven with door slightly ajar 1 hour. Cool to room temperature in pan on wire rack. Cover; refrigerate in pan overnight.

◆ Prepare Black Cat Fudge; do not cut. Using diagram on page 50 as guide, cut out witch shape. Score with knife. Cut small star shapes from scraps with cutter or sharp knife.

◆ Remove cheesecake from side of pan; place on serving plate. Carefully position witch and stars on cheesecake as shown.

Makes 15 servings

continued on page 50

Full-Moon Pumpkin
Cheesecake

Gingersnap Cookie Crust

1 cup gingersnap
   cookie crumbs
½ cup graham cracker
   crumbs
¼ cup sugar
½ cup butter, melted

◆ Preheat oven to 350°F.
Combine cookie crumbs,
cracker crumbs and sugar in
small bowl. Mix in butter.

◆ Press mixture evenly on
bottom and 1 inch up side
of 9-inch springform pan.

◆ Bake 8 minutes; cool on
wire rack.

Makes 1 crust

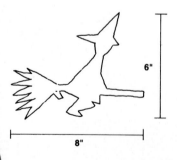

6"

8"

Boo Bites

¼ cup (½ stick) butter
30 large marshmallows
   or 3 cups
   miniature
   marshmallows
¼ cup light corn syrup
½ cup REESE'S® Creamy
   Peanut Butter
⅓ cup HERSHEY'S
   Semi-Sweet
   Chocolate Chips
4½ cups crisp rice cereal

1. Line cookie sheet with
wax paper.

2. Melt butter in large
saucepan over low heat. Add
marshmallows. Cook and stir
until marshmallows are
melted. Remove from heat.
Add corn syrup; stir until
well blended. Add peanut
butter and chocolate chips;
stir until chips are melted
and mixture is well blended.

3. Add cereal; stir until
evenly coated. Cool slightly.
With wet hands, shape
mixture into 1½-inch balls;
place balls on prepared
cookie sheet. Cool
completely. Store in tightly
covered container in cool,
dry place.

Makes 4 dozen pieces

Black Cat Fudge

8 ounces semisweet
    chocolate, chopped
¼ cup butter
⅓ cup light corn syrup
¼ cup whipping cream
1 teaspoon vanilla
¼ teaspoon salt
4½ cups powdered
    sugar, sifted
30 vanilla milk chips

◆ Line 11×7-inch pan with foil, extending foil beyond edges of pan; grease foil.

◆ Melt chocolate and butter in medium saucepan over low heat; stir in corn syrup, cream, vanilla and salt. Remove from heat and gradually stir in powdered sugar until smooth.

◆ Spread evenly in prepared pan. Refrigerate until firm, 1 to 2 hours.

◆ Using foil as handles, remove fudge from pan; peel off foil. Using diagram as guide, cut out cats. Frequently clean knife with warm water and dry thoroughly to prevent sticking. Place 2 vanilla milk chips on each cat for eyes. Score feet to make claws. Cover; refrigerate until ready to serve.

Makes 1½ pounds
(12 to 15 cats)

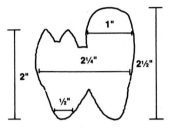

If weather permits, a treasure hunt in the back yard is a great party activity. Some fun prizes to hide are decorated pencils and erasers, stickers, pennies, wrapped candies and small toys, such as spider rings.

Boo the Ghost

1 (13×9-inch) cake, completely cooled
2 cups Light & Fluffy Frosting (recipe follows)
2 black licorice drops or jelly beans

SUPPLIES
1 (19×13) cake board, cut in half crosswise and covered
Plastic spiders (optional)

◆ If cake top is rounded, trim horizontally with long serrated knife. Trim sides of cake.

◆ Using photo as guide, draw ghost outline on 13×9-inch piece of waxed paper. Cut pattern out and place on cake. Cut out ghost. Place on prepared cake board.

◆ Prepare Light & Fluffy Frosting. Frost ghost, swirling frosting. Arrange licorice drops for eyes and spiders as shown in photo.
Makes 14 servings

Light & Fluffy Frosting

⅔ cup sugar
2 egg whites*
5 tablespoons light corn syrup
Dash salt
1 teaspoon vanilla

*Use only Grade A clean, uncracked eggs.

◆ Combine sugar, egg whites, corn syrup and salt in top of double boiler or stainless steel bowl. Set over boiling water. Beat constantly until stiff peaks form, about 7 minutes. Remove from water and beat in vanilla.
Makes about 2 cups

Boo the Ghost

Black Cat Cookies

1 package (18 ounces)
    refrigerated sugar
    cookie dough
White Decorator
    Icing (recipe
    follows)
Black paste food
    coloring
Assorted colored
    candies

◆ Preheat oven to 350°F.
Remove dough from
wrapper according to
package directions. Divide
dough into 2 equal sections.
Reserve 1 section; cover and
refrigerate remaining
section.

◆ Roll reserved dough on
lightly floured surface to ⅛-
inch thickness. Sprinkle with
flour to minimize sticking, if
necessary.

◆ Cut out cookies using 3½-
inch cat face cookie cutter.
Place cookies 2 inches apart
on ungreased baking sheets.
Repeat with remaining
dough and scraps.

◆ Bake 8 to 10 minutes or
until firm but not browned.
Cool on baking sheets 2
minutes. Remove to wire
rack; cool completely.

◆ Prepare White Decorator
Icing. Add desired amount of
food coloring to make black.
Decorate cookies with icing
and assorted candies as
shown in photo.
Makes 20 cookies

White Decorator Icing

4 cups powdered sugar
½ cup vegetable
    shortening or
    unsalted butter
1 tablespoon corn
    syrup
6 to 8 tablespoons milk

◆ Beat sugar, shortening,
corn syrup and milk in
medium bowl 2 minutes or
until fluffy.

Black Cat Cookies

Candy Corn Cookies

Butter Cookie Dough (recipe follows)
Cookie Glaze (recipe follows)
Yellow and orange food colors

◆ Preheat oven to 350°F. Roll dough on floured surface to ¼-inch thickness. Cut out 3-inch candy corn shapes. Place cutouts on ungreased cookie sheets.

◆ Bake 8 to 10 minutes or until edges are browned. Remove to wire racks to cool. Prepare Cookie Glaze.

◆ Place racks over waxed-paper-lined baking sheets. Divide Cookie Glaze among three small bowls. Color ⅓ glaze with yellow food color and ⅓ with orange food color. Leave remaining glaze white. Spoon glazes over cookies to resemble "candy corn." Let stand until set.
Makes 24 cookies

Butter Cookie Dough

¾ **cup butter, softened**
¼ **cup granulated sugar**
¼ **cup packed light brown sugar**
1 **egg yolk**
1¾ **cups all-purpose flour**
¾ **teaspoon baking powder**
⅛ **teaspoon salt**

◆ Mix butter, sugars and egg yolk in medium bowl. Add flour, baking powder and salt; mix well. Cover; chill about 4 hours or until firm.

Cookie Glaze: Mix 4 cups powdered sugar and ¼ cup milk in bowl. Add 1 to 2 tablespoons more milk as needed to make pourable glaze.

Bat Cookies: Omit yellow and orange food colors. Prepare recipe as directed except use bat cookie cutter to cut out cookies. Bake as directed. Color glaze with black paste food color; spoon over cookies. Decorate as desired.

Top to bottom: Bat Cookies and Candy Corn Cookies

Scarecrow Cupcakes

1¼ cups all-purpose
    flour
¾ teaspoon baking
    powder
½ teaspoon baking
    soda
¼ teaspoon salt
¾ teaspoon ground
    cinnamon
⅛ teaspoon each
    ground cloves,
    ground nutmeg
    and ground
    allspice
¾ cup heavy cream
2 tablespoons molasses
¼ cup butter, softened
¼ cup granulated sugar
¼ cup packed brown
    sugar
2 eggs
½ teaspoon vanilla
¾ cup sweetened
    shredded coconut
    Maple Buttercream
    Frosting (page 60)
    Toasted coconut,
    chow mein
    noodles, shredded
    wheat cereal,
    candy corn, mini
    candy-coated
    chocolate pieces,
    gumdrops and
    decorator gel

◆ Preheat oven to 350°F.
Line 18 (2¾-inch) muffin
cups with paper baking
liners. Combine flour, baking
powder, baking soda, salt
and spices in medium bowl;
set aside. Combine cream
and molasses in small bowl;
set aside.

◆ Beat butter in large bowl
until creamy. Add sugars;
beat until light and fluffy.
Add eggs, one at a time,
beating well after each
addition. Blend in vanilla.

◆ Add flour mixture
alternately with cream
mixture to butter mixture,
beating well after each
addition. Stir in coconut;
spoon batter into prepared
muffin cups, filling about
half full.

◆ Bake 20 to 25 minutes or
until toothpick inserted in
centers comes out clean.
Cool in pan on wire rack 10
minutes. Remove cupcakes
to racks; cool completely.

◆ Prepare Maple
Buttercream Frosting. Frost
cupcakes and decorate to
make scarecrow faces as
shown in photo.

Makes 18 servings

continued on page 60

Scarecrow Cupcakes

*Scarecrow Cupcakes,
continued*

Maple Buttercream Frosting

2 tablespoons butter,
   softened
2 tablespoons maple or
   pancake syrup
1½ cups powdered sugar

◆ Beat butter and syrup in
medium bowl until blended.
Gradually beat in powdered
sugar until smooth.
   Makes about 1½ cups

To make a gumdrop hat, roll
out a large gumdrop on a
generously sugared surface.
Cut 1 rounded piece to look like
the top of the hat and 1 straight
piece to look like the brim of
the hat as shown in the photo
on page 59. Overlap the pieces
to make the hat; pipe decorator
gel over the seam for the hat
band.

Spooky Ghost Cookies

1 recipe Butter Cookie
   dough (page 56)
1 recipe Fluffy White
   Frosting (page 46)
½ cup semisweet
   chocolate chips
   (about 60 chips)

◆ Preheat oven to 350°F.
Roll dough on floured
surface to ¼-inch thickness.
Cut out ghost shapes.

◆ Bake on ungreased
cookie sheets 10 to 12
minutes or until edges begin
to brown. Remove to wire
racks; cool completely.

◆ Prepare Fluffy White
Frosting. Spread frosting
over cookies, swirling to
give ghostly appearance.
Position 2 chocolate chips
on each cookie for eyes.
   Makes 30 cookies

Chocolate-Dipped Caramel Apples

1 package (14 ounces) caramels
1 tablespoon water
6 medium apples
4 ounces milk or semisweet chocolate confectionary coating, coarsely chopped
White decorating icing
Candy corn, gummy worms and assorted candies

SUPPLIES
6 wooden craft sticks

◆ Line baking sheet with waxed paper. Unwrap caramels. Combine caramels and water in medium saucepan; cook over medium heat, stirring constantly, until caramels are melted.

◆ Rinse and thoroughly dry apples; insert wooden sticks into stem ends. Dip apples, 1 at a time, into caramel mixture, coating completely. Remove excess caramel mixture by scraping apple bottom across rim of saucepan. Place on waxed paper.

◆ Place confectionary coating in small saucepan. Cook over low heat, stirring frequently, until coating is melted. Dip apples halfway into coating. Return to waxed paper.

◆ Use icing to write names on apples. Use small amount of additional icing to secure desired decorations on apples. Refrigerate until firm.   *Makes 6 servings*

Haunted Hint

Not only can these apples guide your guests to their seats, they make a yummy take-home treat! Simply wrap them up in plastic wrap and tie with black and orange ribbons.

Jack-O'-Lantern

Buttercream Frosting (recipe follows)
Orange, green and brown food colors
2 (10-inch) Bundt cakes
Candy corn

SUPPLIES
2 (10-inch) round cake boards, stacked and covered, or large plate
1 (6-ounce) paper cup or ice cream cone
Pastry bag and medium writing tip

◆ Prepare 2 recipes Buttercream Frosting. Tint 4½ cups frosting orange, ½ cup dark green and ¼ cup dark brown. To tint frosting, add small amount of desired food color; stir well. Slowly add more color until desired shade.

◆ Trim flat sides of cakes. Place one cake on prepared cake board, flat-side up. Frost top of cake with some orange frosting. Place second cake, flat-side down, over frosting.

◆ Frost entire cake with orange frosting.

◆ Hold cup over fingers of one hand. Using other hand, frost cup with green frosting. Place upside-down in center of cake as stem.

◆ Using writing tip and brown frosting, pipe eyes and mouth. Arrange candy corn for teeth. Remove stem before serving.

Makes 40 servings

Buttercream Frosting

6 cups powdered sugar, sifted and divided
¾ cup butter, softened
¼ cup shortening
6 to 8 tablespoons milk, divided
1 teaspoon vanilla

◆ Combine half of sugar, butter, shortening, 4 tablespoons milk and vanilla in large bowl. Beat until smooth. Add remaining sugar; beat until fluffy, adding more milk, 1 tablespoon at a time, as needed for easy spreading.

Makes about 3½ cups

Jack-O'-Lantern

Chocolate Spider Web Cake

1⅔ cups all-purpose
    flour
1½ cups sugar
 ½ cup HERSHEY'S
    Cocoa
1½ teaspoons baking
    soda
 1 teaspoon salt
 ½ teaspoon baking
    powder
 2 eggs
1½ cups buttermilk or
    sour milk*
 ½ cup shortening (do
    not use butter,
    margarine, spread
    or oil)
 1 teaspoon vanilla
    extract
    One-Bowl
    Buttercream
    Frosting (page 66)
    Spider Web (page 66)

*To sour milk: Use 4½ teaspoons
white vinegar plus milk to
equal 1½ cups.

1. Heat oven to 350°F.
Thoroughly grease and flour
two 9-inch round baking
pans.

2. Combine dry ingredients
in large bowl; add eggs,
buttermilk, shortening and
vanilla. Beat on low speed of
mixer 1 minute, scraping
bowl constantly. Beat on
high speed 3 minutes,
scraping bowl occasionally.
Pour batter into prepared
pans.

3. Bake 30 to 35 minutes or
until wooden pick inserted
in centers comes out clean.
Cool 10 minutes; remove
from pans to wire racks.
Cool completely.

4. Frost with One-Bowl
Buttercream Frosting.
Immediately pipe or drizzle
Spider Web in 4 or 5 circles
on top of cake. Using a knife
or wooden pick,
immediately draw 8 to 10
lines from center to edges of
cake at regular intervals to
form web. Garnish with
"spider," using cookie,
licorice and other candies.

Makes 12 servings

continued on page 66

Chocolate Spider Web Cake

*Chocolate Spider Web Cake,
continued*

One-Bowl Buttercream Frosting

> 6 tablespoons butter or
> margarine,
> softened
> 2⅔ cups powdered sugar
> ½ cup HERSHEY'S
> Cocoa
> 4 to 6 tablespoons milk
> 1 teaspoon vanilla
> extract

Beat butter; add powdered
sugar and cocoa alternately
with milk, beating to
spreading consistency. Stir in
vanilla.

Makes about 2 cups

Spider Web: Place ½ cup
HERSHEY'S Premier White
Chips and ½ teaspoon
shortening (do not use
butter, margarine, spread or
oil) in small heavy seal-top
plastic bag. Microwave at
HIGH (100%) 45 seconds.
Squeeze gently. If necessary,
microwave an additional 10
to 15 seconds; squeeze until
chips are melted. With
scissors, make small diagonal
cut in bottom corner of bag;
squeeze mixture onto cake
as directed.

Funny Bug

> 1 (3-inch) oatmeal
> cookie
> 1 tablespoon Fluffy
> White Frosting
> (page 46)
> 2 miniature chocolate
> sandwich cookies
> 1 red gumdrop
> 2 cheese corn curls

Frost oatmeal cookie with
Fluffy White Frosting.
Arrange sandwich cookies
to make eyes. Attach
gumdrop mouth and corn
curl antennae.

Makes 1 cookie

**Clockwise from top left:
Funny Bugs, Spider (page 46),
Spooky Ghost Cookies
(page 60) and Bloodshot
Eyeballs (page 72)**

Monster Munch

6 squares (2 ounces
  each) almond bark,
  divided
1½ cups pretzel sticks
  Orange food coloring
2 cups graham cereal
¾ cup Halloween
  colored candy-
  coated chocolate
  pieces
¾ cup miniature
  marshmallows
½ cup chocolate
  sprinkles

◆ Place 1½ squares almond bark in small microwavable bowl. Microwave at MEDIUM (50% power) 1 minute; stir. Repeat steps as necessary, stirring at 15-second intervals, until completely melted.

◆ Place pretzel sticks in large bowl. Add melted almond bark and stir until all pieces are coated. Spread coated pretzel sticks out on waxed paper, separating individual pieces; let set.

◆ Place remaining 4½ squares almond bark in medium microwavable bowl. Microwave at MEDIUM (50% power) 1 minute; stir. Repeat steps as necessary, stirring at 15-second intervals, until completely melted. Stir in food coloring until almond bark is bright orange.

◆ Place cereal in large bowl. Add half of orange-colored almond bark and stir until cereal is evenly coated. Add chocolate pieces, marshmallows and remaining almond bark; stir until mix is evenly coated. Stir in pretzel sticks.

◆ Break mix into small clusters and spread out on waxed paper. Sprinkle clusters with chocolate sprinkles; let set.

Makes 5 cups mix

Tombstone Place Cards

1 cup vanilla frosting
8 (2×1¼-inch) fudge-coated graham cracker cookies
8 fun-size (2-inch) milk-chocolate-covered caramel candy bars
1 cup chocolate frosting
4 whole graham crackers
8 pumpkin candies
½ cup sweetened shredded coconut, tinted green*

SUPPLIES
Pastry bag and small writing tip

*Dilute a few drops green food color with ¼ teaspoon water in large plastic bag. Add ½ cup flaked coconut. Seal bag and shake well until coconut is evenly tinted.

◆ Spoon vanilla frosting into pastry bag fitted with writing tip; use to write names on fudge-coated graham cracker cookies.

◆ Cover tops of candy bars with small amount of chocolate frosting; stand fudge-coated graham crackers upright on candy bars to form tombstone shapes.

◆ Break graham crackers in half crosswise; spread tops with chocolate frosting. Position candy tombstones and pumpkins in chocolate frosting on graham crackers; sprinkle with coconut to resemble grass.

Makes 8 place cards

Get everyone involved in your Halloween party! Have adults or older kids dress up in scary costumes and be camouflaged in the haunted setting. They can pop out at a pre-arranged time for maximum frightfulness.

Ghoulish Delights

Skull & Cross Bones

1 package (21.5 ounces) brownie mix plus
  ingredients to prepare mix
1 egg white
⅛ teaspoon almond extract, optional
¼ cup sugar
  Red and black decorator gel
1 tub (16 ounces) chocolate frosting

SUPPLIES
  Pastry bag with medium writing tip

◆ Prepare and bake brownies in 13×9-inch baking pan according to package directions. Cool completely.

◆ Preheat oven to 250°F. Line baking sheet with parchment paper; set aside.

continued on page 72

Skull & Cross Bones

*Skull & Cross Bones,
continued*

◆ Beat egg white in large bowl until foamy. Add almond extract, if desired; beat until soft peaks form. Gradually add sugar; beat until stiff peaks form.

◆ Fill pastry bag with egg white mixture. Pipe 24 skull and cross bones shapes onto prepared baking sheet. Bake about 12 minutes or until very lightly browned and set. Cool on pan on wire racks. Carefully remove meringues from parchment paper. Decorate with red gel for eyes and black gel for mouths.

◆ Frost brownies and cut into 24 rectangles. Place one meringue on each brownie.
Makes 24 brownies

Bloodshot Eyeballs

2 fudge-covered chocolate sandwich cookies
1 tablespoon Fluffy White Frosting (page 46)
2 green jelly beans Red decorating gel

Frost cookies with Fluffy White Frosting, leaving edge of cookie showing. Press jelly beans into frosting to make pupils of eyes. Decorate with red gel to make eyes look bloodshot.
Makes 2 eyeballs

The Big Spider Web

- 1½ cups all-purpose flour
- ½ teaspoon baking soda
- ¾ cup creamy peanut butter
- ½ cup margarine or butter, softened
- 1¼ cups firmly packed light brown sugar
- 2 teaspoons vanilla extract
- 1 egg
- ¾ cup milk chocolate chips, divided
- ½ cup PLANTERS® Dry Roasted Peanuts, chopped
- 1 cup marshmallow fluff
  Assorted candies and gummy creatures

Combine flour and baking soda; set aside.

In large bowl, with electric mixer at medium speed, beat peanut butter, margarine, sugar and vanilla until creamy. Beat in egg until light and fluffy; gradually blend in flour mixture. Stir in ½ cup chocolate chips and chopped peanuts.

Press dough into greased 14-inch pizza pan. Bake at 350°F for 20 to 25 minutes or until done. Cool completely in pan on wire rack. Frost top of cookie with marshmallow fluff to within 1-inch of edge. Melt remaining ¼ cup chocolate chips; drizzle in circular pattern over marshmallow. Draw knife through marshmallow topping to create web effect. Decorate with assorted candies and gummy creatures.

Makes 16 servings

Arrange a "boo-tiful" buffet table. Roll up utensils in a festive napkin and use a Halloween cookie cutter as a napkin ring. To keep utensils in easy reach, set them in a black plastic cauldron placed near the plates.

Witch Cake

1 package (2-layer size)
    cake mix, any
    flavor, plus
    ingredients to
    prepare mix
2 tubs (16 ounces each)
    vanilla frosting
    Green food color
    Black decorating gel
    Black food color
    Red licorice whips
1 sugar cone
    Red chewy fruit
    snack and assorted
    candies

SUPPLIES
1 (15×10-inch) cake
    board, covered, or
    large tray
    Pastry bag and
    medium star tip
1 purchased black
    party hat

◆ Preheat oven to 350°F.
Grease and flour 13×9-inch
baking pan.

◆ Prepare cake mix
according to package
directions; pour batter into
prepared pan.

◆ Bake 30 to 35 minutes or
until toothpick inserted in
center comes out clean.
Cool in pan on wire rack

10 minutes. Remove from
pan to rack; cool completely.

◆ If cake top is rounded,
trim horizontally with long
serrated knife. Place cake on
prepared cake board. Spread
top and sides of cake with 1
tub frosting. Transfer about
half of remaining tub
frosting to bowl; tint with
green food color.

◆ Using photo as guide,
trace outline of witch's head
onto frosted cake with
toothpick. Fill in face with
thin layer of green frosting;
outline with decorating gel.

◆ Place remaining frosting
in another small bowl; tint
with black food color. Spoon
into pastry bag fitted with
star tip; pipe frosting around
bottom edges of cake.

◆ Cut hat in half
lengthwise. Place one half
on cake; discard remaining
half. Cut licorice into desired
lengths; place around hat to
resemble hair.

◆ Place sugar cone on cake
for nose. Use candies and
fruit snack cutouts to make
eyes and mouth.
                    Makes 12 servings

Coffin Cookies

1 package (18 ounces)
  refrigerated
  chocolate cookie
  dough*
1 cup vanilla frosting
¾ cup marshmallow
  creme
Assorted sprinkles,
  colored sugars,
  prepared white
  icing and decors

*If refrigerated chocolate
cookie dough is unavailable,
add ¼ cup unsweetened cocoa
powder to refrigerated sugar
cookie dough. Beat in large
bowl until well blended.

◆ Draw pattern for coffin
on cardboard following
diagram; cut out pattern.

◆ Preheat oven to 350°F.
Remove dough from
wrapper. Divide dough into
2 equal sections. Reserve 1
section; cover and chill
remaining section.

◆ Roll reserved dough on
lightly floured surface to ⅛-
inch thickness. Sprinkle with
flour to minimize sticking, if
necessary.

◆ Place pattern on cookie
dough; cut dough around
pattern with sharp knife.

Repeat as necessary. Place
cookies 2 inches apart on
ungreased baking sheets.
Repeat with remaining
dough and scraps.

◆ Bake about 6 minutes or
until firm but not browned.
Cool on baking sheets 2
minutes. Remove to wire
rack; cool completely.

◆ Combine frosting and
marshmallow creme in small
bowl. Spread half of cookies
with 2 teaspoons filling
each; top with remaining
cookies. Roll sandwich
edges in sprinkles.

◆ Decorate with icing and
assorted decors as desired.
Makes about 2 dozen
sandwich cookies

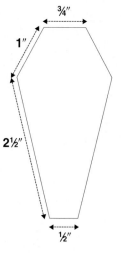

Coffin Cookies

Graveyard Treat

2¼ cups chocolate wafer
     cookie crumbs,
     divided
½ cup sugar, divided
½ cup (1 stick)
     margarine or
     butter, melted
1 package (8 ounces)
     PHILADELPHIA®
     Cream Cheese,
     cubed, softened
1 tub (12 ounces)
     COOL WHIP®
     Whipped Topping,
     thawed
2 cups boiling water
1 package (8-serving
     size) or 2 packages
     (4-serving size)
     JELL-O® Brand
     Orange Flavor
     Gelatin Dessert
½ cup cold water
     Ice cubes
     Rectangular or oval-
     shaped sandwich
     cookies
     Decorator icings
     Candy corn and
     pumpkins

MIX 2 cups of the cookie
crumbs, ¼ cup of the sugar
and the melted margarine
with fork in 13×9-inch
baking pan until crumbs are
well moistened. Press firmly
onto bottom of pan; chill.

BEAT cream cheese and
remaining ¼ cup sugar in
medium bowl with wire
whisk until smooth. Gently
stir in ½ of the whipped
topping. Spread over crust.

STIR boiling water into
gelatin in medium bowl 2
minutes or until completely
dissolved. Mix cold water
and ice cubes to make 1½
cups. Add to gelatin; stir until
slightly thickened
(consistency of unbeaten
egg whites). Remove any
remaining ice. Spoon gelatin
over cream cheese layer.

REFRIGERATE 3 hours or
until firm. Spread remaining
whipped topping over
gelatin just before serving;
sprinkle with remaining ¼
cup cookie crumbs.
Decorate sandwich cookies
with icings to make
"tombstones." Stand
tombstones on top of
dessert with candies to
resemble a graveyard. Cut
into squares to serve.

*Makes 15 to
18 servings*

Graveyard Treat

Orange Jack-O'-Lanterns

6 oranges
1 package (5 ounces) cook-and-serve chocolate pudding mix
2¼ cups milk
1 cup mini semisweet chocolate chips
4 ounces cream cheese, softened and cut into ½-inch cubes
½ teaspoon orange extract
Green Cream Cheese Frosting (recipe follows)
Green Slivered Almonds (recipe follows)

SUPPLIES
Pastry bag with leaf tip

◆ Cut tops from oranges; discard. Scoop out fruit and membranes; reserve for another use. With sharp knife, cut out jack-o'-lantern faces in sides of oranges.

◆ Combine pudding mix and milk in saucepan. Cook and stir over medium heat until pudding comes to a boil. Remove from heat. Add chocolate chips, cream cheese and extract; stir until chips are melted. Cool.

◆ Spoon pudding mixture into oranges. Cover lightly with plastic wrap; refrigerate several hours or overnight.

◆ When ready to serve, spoon Green Cream Cheese Frosting into pastry bag fitted with leaf tip; pipe onto pudding for pumpkin leaves. Add almonds for stems.
Makes 6 servings

Green Cream Cheese Frosting: Beat 4 ounces cream cheese and 2 tablespoons powdered sugar in small bowl until well blended. Tint with green food color. Makes about ½ cup.

Green Slivered Almonds: Place 6 slivered almonds in small resealable plastic food storage bag. Add ⅛ teaspoon green food color; seal bag. Shake bag until almonds are evenly colored. Place almonds on paper-towel-lined plate; let dry.

Smucker's®
Spider Web
Tartlets

1 16-ounce log
   refrigerated sugar
   cookie dough
¾ cup flour
   Nonstick cooking
   spray or
   parchment paper
1 cup (12-ounce jar)
   SMUCKER'S®
   Apricot Preserves
1 tube black cake
   decorating gel

1. Preheat the oven to
375°F. Unwrap cookie dough
and place in medium mixing
bowl. With floured hands,
knead flour into cookie
dough. Roll dough back into
log shape, place on clean
cutting board and cut into
eight equal slices. With
floured fingers, place dough
circles on baking sheet lined
with parchment paper or
sprayed with nonstick spray.

2. Gently press dough
circles, flattening to make
each one approximately 4
inches in diameter. With
thumb and forefinger, pinch
the edge of each dough
circle to create a ridge all

around. Pinch each dough
circle along the ridge to
make eight points.

3. Spread 2 tablespoons of
Smucker's® Jam (or Simply
Fruit) onto each dough
circle, making sure to spread
it all the way to the edges
and in the points. Refrigerate
for 20 minutes. Bake 12 to
14 minutes or until edges
are lightly browned.

4. Remove tartlets from
baking sheet and cool on
wire rack. When cool, use
the black decorating gel to
make a spider web design.
                    Makes 8 servings

For a really eerie setting,
replace regular light bulbs
with black, strobe or colored
light bulbs. Then arrange false
cobwebs on and around the
lamp shades to create some
menacing shadows.

Yummy Mummy Cookies

⅔ cup butter or
    margarine,
    softened
1 cup sugar
2 teaspoons vanilla
    extract
2 eggs
2½ cups all-purpose
    flour
½ cup HERSHEY'S
    Cocoa
¼ teaspoon baking
    soda
½ teaspoon salt
1 cup HERSHEY'S MINI
    CHIPS™ Semi-
    Sweet Chocolate
1 to 2 packages
    (10 ounces each)
    HERSHEY'S
    Premier White
    Chips
1 to 2 tablespoons
    shortening (do *not*
    use butter,
    margarine, spread
    or oil)
    Additional
    HERSHEY'S MINI
    CHIPS™ Semi-
    Sweet Chocolate

1. Beat butter, sugar and vanilla in large bowl until creamy. Add eggs; beat well. Stir together flour, cocoa, baking soda and salt; gradually add to butter mixture, beating until blended. Stir in 1 cup Mini Chips. Refrigerate dough 15 to 20 minutes or until firm enough to handle.

2. Heat oven to 350°F.

3. To form mummy body, using 1 tablespoon dough, roll into 3½-inch carrot shape; place on ungreased cookie sheet. To form head, using 1 teaspoon dough, roll into ball the size and shape of a grape; press onto wide end of body. Repeat procedure with remaining dough.

4. Bake 8 to 9 minutes or until set. Cool slightly; remove from cookie sheet to wire rack. Cool completely.

5. Place 1⅔ cups (10-ounce package) white chips and 1 tablespoon shortening in microwave-safe pie plate or shallow bowl. Microwave at HIGH (100%) 1 minute; stir until chips are melted.

continued on page 84

Yummy Mummy Cookies

Yummy Mummy Cookies,
continued

6. Coat tops of cookies by placing one cookie at a time on table knife or narrow metal spatula; spoon white chip mixture evenly over cookie to coat. (If mixture begins to thicken, return to microwave for a few seconds). Place coated cookies on wax paper. Melt additional chips with shortening, if needed, for additional coating. As coating begins to set on cookies, using a toothpick, score lines and facial features into coating to resemble mummy. Place 2 Mini Chips on each cookie for eyes. Store, covered, in cool, dry place.

Makes about
30 cookies

Macho Monster Cake

1 package
    (18.25 ounces)
    cake mix (any
    flavor) plus
    ingredients to
    prepare mix
1 tub (16 ounces)
    vanilla frosting
    Green and yellow
    food color
    Black decorating gel
1 white chocolate
    baking bar
    (2 ounces)

SUPPLIES
1 (13×9-inch) cake
    board, covered

◆ Preheat oven to 350°F. Grease and flour 13×9-inch baking pan.

◆ Prepare mix according to package directions. Pour into prepared pan. Bake 30 to 35 minutes until toothpick inserted in center comes out clean. Cool in pan on wire rack 10 minutes. Remove from pan to rack; cool.

continued on page 86

Macho Monster Cake

*Macho Monster Cake,
continued*

◆ Tint frosting with green and yellow food color to make ugly monster green as shown in photo on page 85. If cake top is rounded, trim horizontally with long serrated knife. Using Diagram 1 as guide, draw pattern pieces on waxed paper. Cut pieces out; place on cake. Cut around pattern pieces with knife. Remove and discard pattern pieces.

◆ Position pieces on prepared cake board as shown in Diagram 2, connecting with some frosting. Frost cake. Using decorating gel, pipe eyes, mouth, hair and scars. Break white chocolate baking bar into irregular pieces; position inside mouth as teeth.

Makes 12 servings

Note: For cleaner cutting lines and fewer crumbs, place the cooled cake in the freezer for 30 to 45 minutes before cutting.

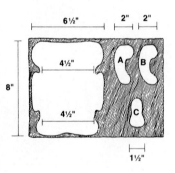

Diagram 1

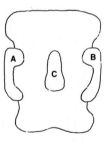

Diagram 2

Chocolate Spiders

¼ cup butter
1 package (12 ounces) semisweet chocolate chips
1 cup butterscotch-flavored chips
¼ cup creamy peanut butter
4 cups crisp rice cereal
Chow mein noodles and assorted candies

◆ Line baking sheet with waxed paper.

◆ Combine butter, chocolate chips and butterscotch chips in large saucepan; stir over medium heat until chips are melted and mixture is well blended. Remove from heat. Add peanut butter; mix well. Add cereal; stir to evenly coat.

◆ Drop mixture by tablespoonfuls, onto prepared baking sheet; insert chow mein noodles for legs and add candies for eyes.

Makes 3 dozen treats

Doughnut Hole Spiders: Substitute chocolate-covered doughnut holes for shaped cereal mixture. Insert black string licorice, cut into 1½-inch lengths, into doughnut holes for legs. Use desired color decorating icing to dot onto doughnut holes for eyes.

Haunted Hint

If your party is in the back yard or basement, have guests enter at the front door of the house and go through a maze of furniture, cardboard or sheets to get to the entrance of the party. Make the maze creepy with dim lights, terrifying sounds and plenty of cobwebs!

Creepy Cookie Cauldrons

1 package (18 ounces) refrigerated chocolate cookie dough*
All-purpose flour
1 bag (14 ounces) caramels, unwrapped
2 tablespoons milk
1 cup crisp rice cereal
¼ cup mini candy-coated chocolate pieces
Black licorice whips and small gummy insects, frogs or lizards

*If refrigerated chocolate cookie dough is unavailable, add ¼ cup unsweetened cocoa powder to refrigerated sugar cookie dough. Beat in large bowl until well blended.

◆ Grease 36 (1¾-inch) mini muffin cups. Remove dough from wrapper according to package directions. Sprinkle dough with flour to minimize sticking, if necessary.

◆ Cut dough into 36 equal pieces; roll into balls. Place 1 ball in bottom of each muffin cup. Press dough on bottoms and up sides of muffin cups; chill 15 minutes. Preheat oven to 350°F.

◆ Bake 8 to 9 minutes. (Cookies will be puffy.) Remove from oven; gently press down center of each cookie. Return to oven 1 minute. Cool cookies in muffin cups 5 minutes. Remove to wire racks; cool completely.

◆ Melt caramels and milk in small saucepan over low heat, stirring frequently until smooth. Stir in cereal. Spoon 1 heaping teaspoon caramel mixture into each cookie cup. Immediately sprinkle with mini chocolate pieces.

◆ Cut licorice whips into 4½-inch lengths. For each cookie, make small slit in side; insert end of licorice strip. Repeat on other side of cookie to make cauldron handle. Decorate with gummy creatures.
Makes 36 cookies

Creepy Cookie Cauldrons

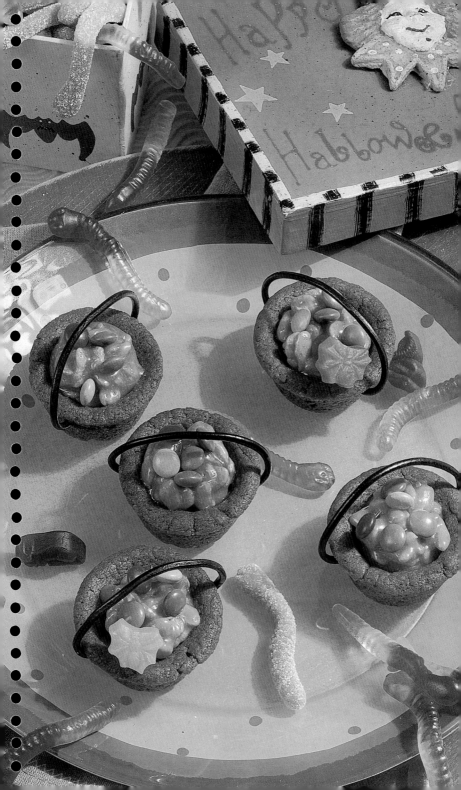

Halloween Haunted House

1 tub (16 ounces) chocolate fudge frosting
Pretzel sticks, nuts, fudge-coated graham crackers, black licorice twists, black jelly beans, sugar wafers, candy corn, dried papaya and other assorted candies

SUPPLIES

2 empty 1-quart milk cartons, rinsed and dried
1 (13×11-inch) cake board, covered, or large tray

◆ Tape each milk carton closed at top. Tape milk cartons together to make house; wrap with foil. Attach securely to covered cake board with tape. Frost cartons and decorate using frosting to attach decorations.

Makes 1 centerpiece

Frozen Witches' Heads

3 whole graham crackers
6 scoops mint-flavored ice cream
6 chocolate-flavored ice cream cones
Red string licorice
Small round candies
Candy corn

◆ Break graham crackers crosswise in half. Place 1 scoop ice cream on center of each cracker; top with inverted ice cream cone for hat.

◆ Cut licorice into 1½-inch lengths; place next to cone for hair. Add candies for eyes and candy corn for noses. Freeze 4 to 6 hours or until firm.   *Makes 6 servings*

Halloween Haunted House

Black Cat Cupcakes

1 package (2-layer size) cake mix (any flavor) plus ingredients to prepare mix
1 tub (16 ounces) chocolate fudge frosting
  Graham crackers
  Assorted candies and black string licorice

◆ Preheat oven to 350°F. Line 24 regular-size (2½-inch) muffin pan cups with paper baking liners. Prepare cake mix according to package directions; spoon into prepared muffin pans.

◆ Bake 15 to 20 minutes until toothpick inserted in centers comes out clean. Cool in pans on wire racks 10 minutes. Remove to racks; cool completely.

◆ Frost tops of cupcakes. With serrated knife, cut graham crackers into small triangles; place on cupcakes for ears. Decorate with candies for eyes and noses, and licorice for whiskers.
Makes 24 cupcakes

Magic Wands

1 cup semisweet chocolate chips
12 pretzel rods
3 ounces white chocolate baking bars
  Orange food color
  Assorted sprinkles

SUPPLIES
  Ribbon

◆ Line baking sheet with waxed paper.

◆ Melt semisweet chocolate in top of double boiler over hot, not boiling, water. Remove from heat. Dip pretzel rods into chocolate, spooning chocolate to coat about ¾ of each pretzel. Place on prepared baking sheet. Chill until firm.

◆ Melt white chocolate in top of clean double boiler over hot, not boiling, water. Stir in food color to make orange. Remove from heat. Dip coated pretzels quickly into colored chocolate to coat about ¼ of each pretzel. Place on baking sheet. Top with sprinkles. Chill until firm. Tie ends with ribbons.
Makes 12 wands

Acknowledgments

The publisher would like to thank the companies and organizations listed below for the use of their recipes and photographs in this publication.

Birds Eye®

Hershey Foods Corporation

Idaho Potato Commission

Kraft Foods, Inc.

Lipton®

Nabisco Biscuit Company
National Chicken Council

PLANTERS® Nuts

The J. M. Smucker Company

Washington Apple Commission

Index